NOTEBOOK M

NOTEBOOK M
gillian savigny

INSOMNIAC PRESS

Copyright © 2012 by Gillian Savigny

Edited for the press by Sachiko Murakami

All rights reserved. No part of this publication may be
reproduced, stored in a retrieval system or transmitted, in any form or by any means, without
the prior written permission of the publisher or, in the case of photocopying or other
reprographic copying, a licence from
Access Copyright, 1 Yonge Street, Suite 1900, Toronto, ON M5E 1E5

Library and Archives Canada Cataloguing in Publication

Savigny, Gillian, 1982-
Notebook M / Gillian Savigny.

Poems.
ISBN 978-1-55483-083-1

I. Title.

PS8637.A875N68 2012   C811'.6   C2012-905390-2

The publisher gratefully acknowledges the support of
the Canada Council, the Ontario Arts Council,
and the Department of Canadian Heritage through the
Canada Book Fund.

Printed and bound in Canada

Insomniac Press
520 Princess Avenue, London, Ontario, Canada, N6B 2B8
www.insomniacpress.com

For Zac and for Margie, Wayne, Meghan, and Allison

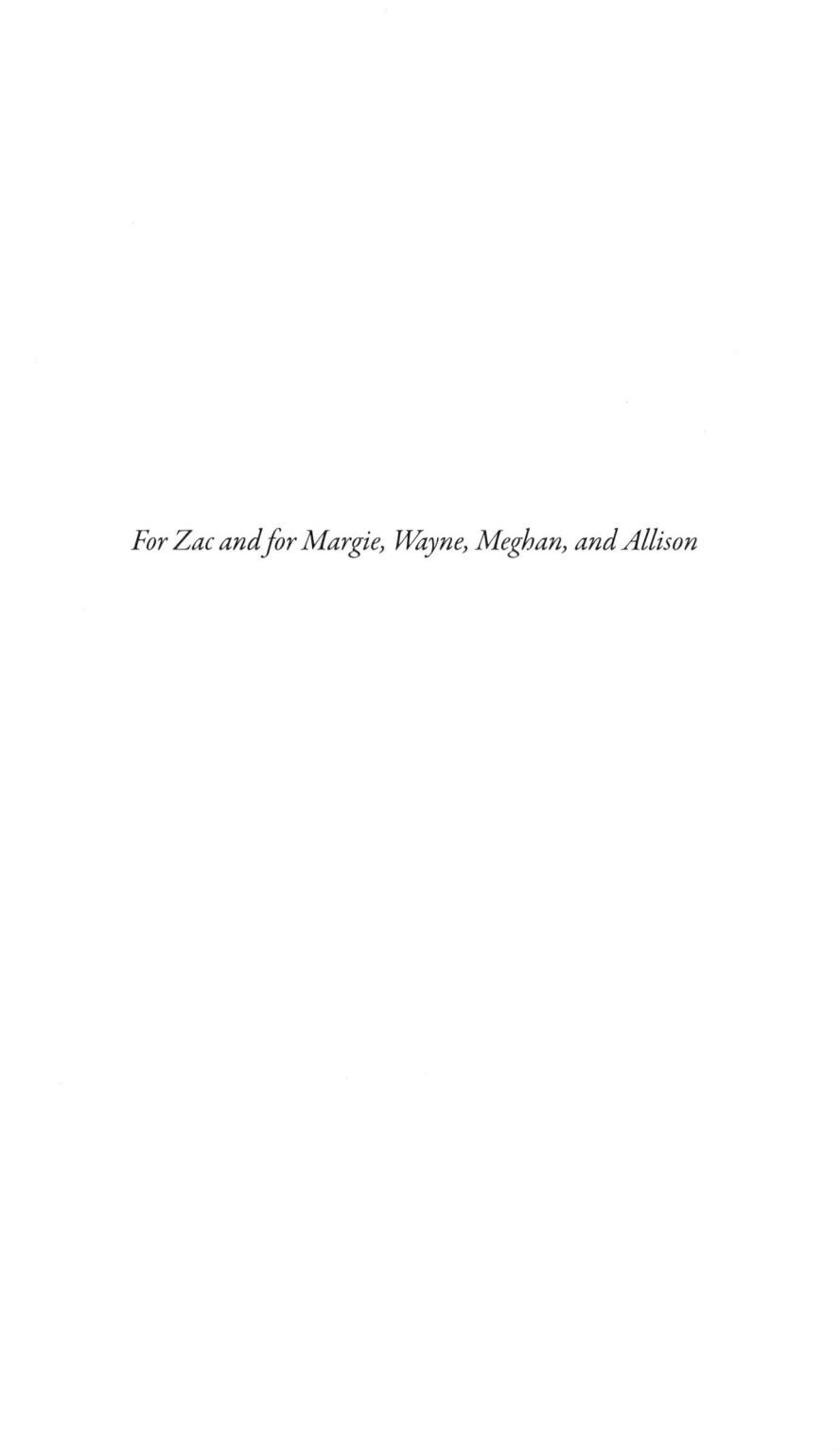

Now that I have a test of hardness of thought, from weakness of my stomach I observe a long castle in the air, is as hard work (abstracting it being done in open air, with exercise &c no organs of sense being required) as the closet train of geological thought.— the capability of such trains of thought makes a discoverer, & therefore (independent of improving powers of invention) such castles in the air are highly advantageous, before real train of inventive thoughts are brought into play & then perhaps the sooner castles in air are banished the better.

    Charles Darwin
    "Notebook M"

CONTENTS

Introduction   11

Darwin   13

Journal of Researches – Patagonia   15

An Autobiographical Fragment   39
Theatre of Memory, an Inventory   41
Three Studies of Fruit   44
Vanitas   48
Death of My Mother   50
The Game Book   51
A Vague Picture of Ships   53
The Laboratory   55

Notebook M   59
Walking Palm   61
The Treehouse   63
Botanist Somnambulist   64
The Sleep of Leaves   65
Paper Birch   66
What the Earth Would Say   67
Envy   68
Petrified Forest   70
M Is for Metaphor   71
M Is for Morality   72
Type Specimen #1   73
Type Specimen #2   75
Type Specimen #3   77

M Is for Metaphysics	79
M Is for Materialism	80
The Empirical Disciplines	81
The Scientific Method	83
M Is for Mania	84
M Is for Memory	85
The Dictionary	86
Tails, Pits, Beaks, and Wings	87
Blind Cave Fish	89
M Is for Monkeys	90
Sources	91
Acknowledgements	93

INTRODUCTION

When Charles Darwin (1809–1882) returned to England after sailing around the world for five years, he began developing, in a series of notebooks, what would become his theory of evolution. From 1836 to the early 1840s, as he established himself as an accomplished naturalist, first in Cambridge then in London, his notebooks recorded a wide range of questions, speculations, conversations, readings, and experiments—the tracks of a relentlessly inquisitive mind intent on demonstrating that the transmutation hypothesis could be used to answer some of the most perplexing questions in biology.

Through the "Red Notebook"; "Notebooks A," "B," "C," "D," and "E"; and the "Torn Apart Notebook," Darwin explored his hypothesis and built the foundation for *On the Origin of Species* (1859), but during the writing of "Notebook C," something happened. More and more Darwin began to explore ideas about human behaviour and the metaphysical and epistemological implications of his developing theory, and so on July 15, 1838, he opened two new notebooks: one he labeled "D" in which he would continue his transmutationist speculations, and another he labeled "M" in which he would explore "Metaphysics on Morals & Speculations on Expression."

The following poems explore what *M* means—metaphysics? morality? memory? metaphor? monkeys?—and the separate mental space the ideas that fall under it are afforded. "Notebook M" and the notebooks that follow in its path—"Notebook N" and "Old and Useless Notes"—display a remarkable creativity at work in Darwin's scientific consciousness. I have tried to reimagine what that creativity might accomplish when given the space to play.

Darwin

left the garden of England
with hardly a hair on his chin.
With God in his heart, the earth in his head, and the sea
in his stomach, he drowned in nausea
from Plymouth to Bahia. He weathered
the rough seas, cloistered in his cabin,
praying for land,
        praying to land.
Off the coast of Patagonia, the ship sailed into a storm
of butterflies so thick the sky was lost behind them,
and Darwin fixed their sea wings to a thought in his mind.
Today: butterflies at sea. Last week: beetles.
In the sea off Cape Corrientes, he hadn't been looking
for insects but found them in the thousands,
and spiders descending with silk parachutes
from some mysterious source.
But since all he ever thought at sea
was land, land, land, he reasoned:
they must come from a land mass,
but there was none for miles,
and miles were too far for spider steps,
and steps were no good on water unless you were God,
and Darwin,
with all that land pounding in his head,
could only think: *spiders, island,*
and maybe the wind.

JOURNAL OF RESEARCHES – PATAGONIA

Rio Plata – Flocks of butterflies – Beetles alive in the sea – Aeronaut spiders – Pelagic animals – Phosphorescence of sea – Port Desire – Spanish settlements – Zoology – Guanaco – Excursion to head of harbour – Indian grave – Port St. Julian – Geology of Patagonia, successive terraces, transport of pebbles – Fossil gigantic llama – Types of organization constant – Change in zoology of America – Causes of extinction.

Such is the history of the changes by which the present condition of Patagonia has, I believe, been determined. These changes all result from the assumption of a steady but very gradual elevation, extending over a wide area and interrupted at long intervals by periods of repose. But we must now return to Port St. Julian. On the south side of the harbour, a cliff of about ninety feet in height intersects a plain constituted of the formations above described, and its surface is strewed over with recent marine shells. The gravel, however, differently from that in every other locality, is covered by a very irregular and thin bed of reddish loam, containing a few small calcareous concretions. The matter somewhat resembles that of the Pampas and probably owes its origin either to a small stream having formerly entered the sea at that spot, or to a mudbank similar to those now existing at the head of the harbour. In one spot, this earthy matter filled up a hollow, or gully, worn quite through the gravel, and in this mass, a group of large bones was embedded. The animal to which they belonged must have lived, as in the case at Bahia Blanca, at a period long subsequent to the existence of the shells now inhabiting the coast. We may feel sure of this, because the formation of the lower terrace or plain must necessarily have been posterior to those above it, and on the surface of the two higher ones, seashells of recent species are scattered. From the small physical change, which the last hundred feet elevation of the continent could have produced, the climate, as well as the general condition of Patagonia, probably was nearly the same at the time when the animal was embedded as it now is. This conclusion is moreover supported by the identity of the shells belonging to the two ages. Then immediately occurred the difficult, how could any large quadruped have subsisted on these wretched deserts in lat. 49° 15'? I had no idea at the time to what kind of animal these remains belonged. The puzzle, however, was soon solved when Mr. Owen examined them, for he considers that they formed part of an animal allied to the guanaco or llama but fully as large as the true camel. As all the existing members of the family of Camelidæ are inhabitants of the most sterile countries, so may we suppose was this extinct kind. The structure of the cervical vertebræ, the transverse processes not being perforated for the vertebral artery, indicates its affinity: some other parts, however, of its structure probably are anomalous.

In such a country, the fate of the Spanish settlement was soon decided; the dryness of the climate during the greater part of the year, and the occasional hostile attacks of the wandering Indians, compelled the colonists to desert their half-finished buildings. The style, however, in which they were commenced showed the strong and liberal hand of Spain in the old time. The end of all the attempts to colonize this side of America south of 41° have been miserable. At Port Famine the name expresses the lingering and extreme suffering of several a hundred wretched people, of whom one alone survived to relate their misfortunes. At St. Joseph's Bay, on the coast of Patagonia, a small settlement was made, but during one Sunday, the Indians made an attack and massacred the whole party, excepting two men who were led captive many years among the wandering tribes. At the Rio Negro, I conversed with one of these men, now in extreme old age. The zoology of Patagonia is as limited as its flora. On the arid plains, a few black beetles (Heteromera) might be seen slowly crawling about, and occasionally a lizard darting from side to side. Of birds, we have three carrion hawks, and in the valleys, a few finches and insect feeders. The *Ibis melanops* (a species said to be found in central Africa) is not uncommon on the most desert parts. In the stomachs of these birds, I found grasshoppers, cicadæ, small lizards, and even scorpions. At one time of the year, they go in flocks, at another, in pairs: their cry is very loud and singular and resembles the neighing of the guanaco. I will here give an account of this latter animal, which is very common and is the characteristic quadruped of the plains of Patagonia. The guanaco, which by some naturalists is considered as the same animal with the llama but in its wild state, is the South American representative of the camel in the East. In size, it may be compared to an ass mounted on taller legs and with a long neck. The guanaco abounds over the whole of the temperate parts of South America, from the wooded islands of Tierra del Fuego through Patagonia; the hilly parts of La Plata, Chile; even to the Cordillera of Peru. Although preferring an elevated site, it yields in this respect to its near relative the vicuna. On the plains of Southern Patagonia, we saw them in greater numbers than in any other part. Generally, they go in small herds, from half a dozen to thirty together, but on the banks of the St. Cruz, we saw one herd that must have contained at least 500. On the northern shores of the Strait of Magellan, they are also very numerous.

It is impossible to reflect without deepest astonishment on the changed state of this continent. Formerly, it must have swarmed with great monsters, like the southern parts of Africa, but now we find only the tapir, guanaco, armadillo, and capybara, mere pigmies compared with the antecedent races. The greater number, if not all, of these extinct quadrupeds lived at a very recent period, and many of them were contemporaries of the existing mollusks. Since their loss, no very great physical changes can have taken place in the nature of the country. What, then, has exterminated so many living creatures? In the Pampas, the great sepulcher of such remains, there are no signs of violence but, on the contrary, of the most quiet and scarcely sensible changes. At Bahia Blanca, I endeavoured to show the probability that the ancient Edentata, like the present species, lived in a dry and sterile country, such as now is found in that neighbourhood. With respect to the camel-like llama of Patagonia, the same grounds that, before knowing more than the size of the remains, perplexed me, by not allowing any great change of climate, now that we can guess the habits of the animal, are strangely confirmed. What shall we say of the death of the fossil horse? Did those plains fail in pasture, which afterwards were overrun by stock introduced with the Spanish colonist? In some countries, we may believe that a number of species subsequently introduced, by consuming the food of the antecedent races, may have caused their extermination, but we can scarcely credit that the armadillo has devoured the food of the immense Megatherium, the capybara of the Toxodon, or the guanaco of the camel-like kind. But granting that all such changes have been small, yet we are so profoundly ignorant concerning the physiological relations on which the life, and even health (as shown by epidemics), of any existing species depends, that we argue with still less safety about either the life or death of any extinct kind.

JANUARY 9th, 1834. – Before it was dark, the *Beagle* anchored in the fine spacious harbour of Port St. Julian, situated about 110 miles to the south of Port Desire. We remained here eight days. The country is nearly similar to that of Port Desire but, perhaps, rather more sterile. One day, a party accompanied Captain FitzRoy on a long walk round the head of the harbour. We were eleven hours without tasting any water, and some of the party were quite exhausted. From the summit of a hill (since well-named Thirsty Hill), a fine lake was spied, and two of the party proceeded with concerted signals to show whether it was fresh water. What was our disappointment to find a snow-white expanse of salt, crystallized in great cubes! We attributed our extreme thirst to the dryness of the atmosphere, but whatever the cause might be, we were exceedingly glad late in the evening to get back to the boats. Although we could nowhere find, during our whole visit, a single drop of fresh water, yet some must exist, for by an odd chance I found on the surface of the salt water, near the head of the bay, a Colymbetes not quite dead, which in all probability had lived in some not far distant pool. Three other insects – a Cincindela, like *hybrida*, a Cymindis, and a Harpalus, which all live on muddy flats occasionally overflowed by the sea, and one other found dead on the plain – complete the list of the Coleoptera. A good-sized fly (Tabanus) was extremely numerous and tormented us by its painful bite. The common horsefly, which is so troublesome in the shady lanes of England, belongs to this same genus. We here have the puzzle that so frequently occurs in the case of mosquitoes: on the blood of what animals do these insects commonly feed? The guanaco is nearly the only warm-blooded quadruped, and it is found in quite inconsiderable numbers compared with the multitude of flies.

The second day after our return to the anchorage, a party of officers and myself went to ransack an old Indian grave, which I had found on the summit of a neighbouring hill. Two immense stones, each probably weighing at least a couple of tons, had been placed in front of a ledge of rock about six feet high. At the bottom of the grave on the hard rock there was a layer of earth about a foot deep, which must have been brought up from the plain below. Above it a pavement of flat stones was placed, on which others were piled so as to fill up the space between the ledge and the two great blocks. To complete the grave, the Indians had contrived to detach from the ledge a huge fragment and to throw it over the pile so as to rest on the two blocks. We undermined the grave on both sides but could not find any relics, or even bones. The latter probably had decayed long since (in which case the grave must have been of extreme antiquity), for I found in another place some smaller heaps beneath which a very few crumbling fragments could yet be distinguished as having belonged to a man. Falconer states that where an Indian dies he is buried but that subsequently his bones are carefully taken up and carried, let the distance be ever so great, to be deposited near the sea coast. This custom, I think, may be accounted for by recollecting that before the introduction of horses, these Indians must have led nearly the same life as the Fuegians now do and therefore generally have resided in the neighbourhood of the sea. The common prejudice of lying where one's ancestors have lain would make the now roaming Indians bring the less perishable part of their dead to their ancient burial ground on the coast.

DECEMBER 6th, 1833 – The *Beagle* sailed from the Rio Plata, never again to enter its muddy stream. Our course was directed to Port Desire, on the coast of Patagonia. Before proceeding any further, I will here put together a few observations made at sea. Several times when the ship has been some miles off the mouth of the Plata, and at other times when off the shores of Northern Patagonia, we have been surrounded by insects. One evening, when we were about ten miles from the Bay of San Blas, vast numbers of butterflies, in bands or flocks of countless myriads, extended as far as the eye could range. Even by the aid of a glass it was not possible to see a space free of butterflies. The seamen cried out "it was snowing butterflies," and such in fact was the appearance. More species than one were present, but the main part belonged to a kind very similar to, but not identical with, the common English *Colias edusa*. Some moths and hymenoptera accompanied the butterflies, and a fine Calosoma flew on board. Other instances are known of this beetle having been caught far out at sea and this is the more remarkable, as the greater number of the Carabidæ seldom or never take wing. The day had been fine and calm, and the one previous to it equally so, with light and variable airs. Hence we cannot suppose that the insects were blown off the land, but we must conclude that they voluntarily took flight. The great bands of the Colias seem at first to afford an instance like those on record of the migrations of *Vanessa cardui*, but the presence of other insects makes the case distinct and not so easily intelligible. Before sunset, a strong breeze sprung up from the north, and this must have been the cause of tens of thousands of the butterflies and other insects having perished.

As we proceed further southward, the sea is seldom phosphorescent, and off Cape Horn, I do not recollect more than once having seen it so, and then it was far from being brilliant. This circumstance probably has a close connexion with the scarcity of organic beings in that part of the ocean. After the elaborate paper by Ehrenberg on the phosphorescence of the sea, it is almost superfluous on my part to make any observations on the subject. I may however add that the same torn and irregular particles of gelatinous matter, described by Ehrenberg, seem in the southern as well as in the northern hemisphere to be the common cause of this phenomenon. The particles were so minute as easily to pass through fine gauze, yet many were distinctly visible by the naked eye. The water when placed in a tumbler and agitated gave out sparks, but a small portion in a watch glass scarcely ever was luminous. Ehrenberg states that these particles all retain a certain degree of irritability. My observations, some of which were made directly after taking up the water, would give a different result. I may also mention, that having used the net during one night, I allowed it to become partially dry, and having occasion twelve hours afterwards to employ it again, I found the whole surface sparkled as brightly as when first taken out of the water. It does not appear probable in this case that the particles could have remained so long alive. I remark also in my notes, that having kept a Medusa of the genus Dianæ till it was dead, the water in which it was placed became luminous. When the waves scintillate with bright green sparks, I believe it is generally owing to minute crustacea. But there can be no doubt that very many other pelagic animals, when alive, are phosphorescent.

One is tempted to believe
variation of climate,
or the increased
of the succession of
it is probable that
action during the same epoch over the
hemisphere so as to destroy the
shores of Spain, on the plains of Siberia, and in
America, and in a like manner, the *bos urus*, over a range of
scarcely less extent? Did such changes put a period to the
life of *Mastodon angustidens*, and of the fossil horse, both
in Europe and on the Eastern slope of the Cordillera in
Southern America? If they did, they must have been changes
common to the whole world, such as gradual refrigeration,
whether from modifications of physical geography, or
from central cooling. But on this assumption, we have to
struggle with the difficulty that these supposed changes,
although scarcely sufficient to affect molluscous animals
either in Europe or South America, yet destroyed many
quadrupeds in regions now characterized by *frigid*, *temperate*,
and *warm* climates! These cases of extinction forcibly recall
the idea (I do not wish to draw any close analogy) of certain
fruit trees, which, it has been asserted, though grafted on
young stems, planted in varied situation, and fertilized by
the richest manures, yet at one period, have all withered
away and perished. A fixed and determined length of life
has in such cases been given to thousands and thousands
of buds (or individual germs), although produced in long
succession. Among the greater number of animals, **each
individual appears** nearly **independent** of its kind, **yet all
of one kind may be bound together by** common laws, as
well as a certain number of individual buds in the **tree**, or
polypi in the zoophyte.

The guanacos appear to have favourite spots for dying in. On the banks of the St. Cruz, the ground was actually white with bones, in certain circumscribed spaces, which were generally bushy and all near the river. On one such spot, I counted between ten and twenty heads. I particularly examined the bones; they did not appear, as some scattered ones which I had seen, gnawed or broken, as if dragged together by beasts of prey. The animals in most cases must have crawled, before dying, beneath and amongst the bushes. Mr. Bynoe informs me that during the last voyage, he observed the same circumstance on the banks of the Rio Gallegos. I do not at all understand the reason of this, but I may observe that the wounded guanacos at the St. Cruz invariably walked towards the river. At St. Jago in the Cape de Verd islands, I remember having seen in a retired ravine a corner under a cliff where numerous goats' bones were collected: we at the time exclaimed that it was the burial ground of all the goats in the island. I mention these trifling circumstances because in certain cases they might explain the occurrence of a number of uninjured bones in a cave, or buried under alluvial accumulations, and likewise the cause why certain mammalian are more commonly embedded than others in sedimentary deposits. Any great flood of the St. Cruz would wash down many bones of the guanaco but probably not a single one of the puma, ostrich, or fox. I may also observe that almost every kind of waterfowl when wounded takes to the shore to die so that the remains of birds, from this cause alone and independently of other reasons, would but rarely be preserved in a fossil state.

During our different passages south of the Plata, I often towed astern a net made of bunting and thus caught many curious animals. The structure of the Beroe (a kind of jellyfish) is most extraordinary, with its rows of vibratory ciliæ and complicated though irregular system of circulation. Of crustacea, there were many strange and undescribed genera. One, which in some respects is allied to the Notopods (or those crabs which have their posterior legs placed almost on their backs for the purpose of adhering to the underside of ledges), is very remarkable from the structure of its hind pair of legs. The penultimate joint, instead of being terminated by a simple claw, ends in three bristle-like appendages of dissimilar lengths, the longest equaling that of the entire leg. These claws are very thin and are serrated with teeth of an excessive fineness, which are directed towards the base. The curved extremities are flattened, and on this part, five most minute cups are placed, which seem to act in the same manner as the suckers on the arms of the cuttlefish. As the animal lives in the open sea, and probably wants a place of rest, I suppose this beautiful structure is adapted to take hold of the globular bodies of the Medusæ, and other floating marine animals.

In deep water far from the land, the number of living creatures is extremely small; south of the latitude 35°, I never succeeded in catching anything besides some beroe and a few species of minute crustacea belonging to the Entomostraca. In shoaler water, at the distance of a few miles from the coast, very many kinds of crustacean and some other animals were numerous, but only during the night. Between latitudes 56° and 57° south of Cape Horn, the net was put astern several times; it never, however, brought up anything besides a few of two extremely minute species of Entomostraca. Yet whales and seal, petrels and albatross, are exceedingly abundant throughout this part of the ocean. It has always been **a source of mystery** to me on what the latter, which live far from the shore, can subsist. I presume the albatross, like the condor, is able to fast long and that one good feast on the carcass of a putrid whale lasts for **a long siege of hunger**. It does not lessen the difficulty to say they feed on fish, for on what can the fish feed? It often occurred to me, when observing how the waters of the central and intertropical parts of the Atlantic, swarmed with Pteropoda, Crustacea, and Radiata, and with their devourers the flying fish, and again with their devourers the bonitos and albacores, that the lowest of these pelagic animals perhaps possess the power of decomposing carbonic acid gas, like the members of the vegetable kingdom.

The same evening I went on shore. The first landing in any new country is very interesting, and especially when, as in this case, the whole aspect bears the stamp of a marked and individual character. At the height of between 200 and 300 feet, above some masses of porphyry, a wide plain extends, which is truly characteristic of Patagonia. The surface is quite level and is composed of well-rounded shingle mixed with a whitish earth. Here and there scattered tufts of brown wiry grass are supported, and still more rarely some low thorny bushes. The weather is dry and pleasant, for the fine blue sky is but seldom obscured. When standing in the middle of one of these desert plains, the view on one side is generally bounded by the escarpment of another plain, rather higher, but equally level and desolate and on the other side it becomes indistinct from the trembling mirage which seems to rise from the heated surface.

The plains are traversed by many broad, flat-bottomed **valleys**, and in these the bushes **grow** rather more **abundantly**. The present drainage of the country is quite insufficient to excavate such large channels. In some of the valleys **ancient stunted trees**, growing in the very centre of the **dry** watercourse, seem **as** if placed to prove how long a **time** had elapsed since any flood had passed that way. **We** have **evidence**, from **shells** lying on the surface, that the plains of gravel have been elevated within a recent epoch above the level of **the sea** and we must look to that period for excavation of the valleys by the slowly retiring **waters**. From the dryness of the climate, a man may walk for days together over these plains **without finding a single drop of water**. Even at the base of the porphyry hills, there are only a few small **wells containing** but little water, **and that rather saline** and half putrid.

We have now stated the problem, which is to be explained so as to connect together these various phenomena. At first I could only understand the grand covering of gravel, by the supposition of some epoch of **extreme violence and** the **success**ive lines **of** cliff, by as many great elevations, **the precise** action of which I could not however follow out. **Guide**d by the "Principles of Geology," and having under my view **the vast changes** going on **in** this continent, which as the present day seems **the** great **workshop of nature** I came to another, and I hope more satisfactory conclusion. The importance of any view which may explain the agency by which such vast beds of shingle **have been** transported over the surface of **the** successive plains, cannot be **doubted. Whatever the cause** may **have been, it has determined** the condition of **this desert country, with respect to its form, nature, and capabilities of supporting life.**

By the middle of the next day the yawl was aground, and from the shoalness of the water could not proceed any higher. The water **being** found partly fresh, Mr. Chaffers took the dingey and went **up** two or three miles further, where she also grounded, but in a fresh-water river. The water was muddy, and though the stream was most insignificant in size **it would be difficult to account for its origin except from the melting snow on** the Cordillera. At the spot where **we** bivouacked, we were surrounded by **bold cliffs** and steep pinnacles of **porph**yry. I do not think I ever saw a **spot** which appeared more secluded **from** the rest of the world, than this **rocky** crevice in the **wide plain**. In the **evening** we sailed a few miles further **up, and** then pitched the tents for the **night.**

read the submarine basis of Patagonia then lift up the pebbles spread out over the bottom of the invading waters.

beneath the ark the animals congregate

we carry gravel a considerable distance from the parent rock a a of ss, a

          in
                    Patagonia

     we

anchor

                    the ruins of
old   men

we

      belong to
the

      ground

An Autobiographical Fragment

We know less than ever where to cut—either at birth or death.
*And this also means that we never know, and never have **known**,*
how to cut up *a subject.*

   Jacques Derrida
   "Eating Well, or the Calculation of the Subject"

Theatre of Memory, an Inventory

The curiosities described below were recovered from the body of the author. Each is listed under the organ in which it was found.

Skull: glow-in-the-dark stars; a shark-tooth necklace comprising twenty-one pieces, each piece being engraved with a letter so that the string reads *Carcharodon carcharias*.

Brain: a colossal dragon tree, sixty feet tall and growing such that if the branches were unfurled they could reach all the way to the moon.

Eyes: various coins of Greek and Roman origin; a tongue extracted from a dog in mid-pant and preserved in a jug of its own saliva.

Trachea: a cactus spine that once got caught in the neck of a finch, changing its voice and the song of its descendants. Note: this ancient injury can still be heard in the spring.

Larynx: a wax seal imprinted with three shells; a dactyl, a trochee, and other metric reptiles; a name that crawled out of the water in Lancashire to make its home among animals.

Lungs: the remains of a giant—an ichthyosaur—tangled among the branches of the bronchial tree. Note: this is where his grandfather is buried.

Heart: a piece of the great Map of the Empire resting in a nest of tumbleweed.

Liver: a vase, a penguin's egg, a letter dated February 1839, wild lilies, and other mild aphrodisiacs.

Stomach: a mammoth tooth and the ear of the ocean.

Pancreas: an instruction book for turning objects into memories written on the skin of a Portuguese man-of-war with the ink of an octopus.

Intestines: the brain of a Tasmanian tiger and an *Equus quagga quagga*.

Appendix: various religious objects: dark nails, incense, gold, bones.

Kidneys: pyrite, feldspar, barnacles, rocks dug up in a field.

Veins: mahogany; blue spruce sap.

Pelvis: a cradle; a botanical encyclopedia, which

has been watered so the pictures of the woolly fern and *Drosera* grow.

Adrenal glands: a wooden spear, missing its head.

Bladder: a windmill; a trap door.

Spleen: a reservoir of blood, a second heart, various spare parts, three litres of melancholy, and a sense of humour.

Mammary glands: phosphorescence used in the manufacture of perfume; two stillborn infants swimming in circles like a pair of goldfish.

Vas deferens: unfinished sculptures attributed to Michelangelo straining to escape their marble.

Hands: antlers; three spiders.

Rib cage: clock gears and an antique cabinet judged to be too decadent.

Three Studies of Fruit

Thinking over the scenes which I first recollect...they are all things, which are brought to mind, by the memory of the scenes, (indeed my American recollections are a collection of pictures)...one is tempted to think all memory consists in a set of sketches, some real—some fancied.

    Charles Darwin
    "Notebook M"

Have I painted these scenes?
Or merely collected them?
I will try to display them
in pure colours, simplest
form.

i.

First: the orange of an orange[1]

*I, four years old,
sitting on Caroline's knee
in the dining room.
She is cutting the fruit for me
when a cow rushes past the window,*
startling me so I startle the knife,

---

[1] My father kept nine orange trees in the hothouse at Shrewsbury—a collection that rivaled the Orangery at Kew.

and it bites[2] my thumb
between the knuckles.

I do not remember the cut itself,
but the pain must have acted like a
flash—citrus spark sting—
illuminating the moment
for my memory to capture.[3]

ii.

The outline of a house
and a small shop.

The house I am staying in
while on vacation with my family,
and the shop contains a shopkeeper
who gave me one fig[4] so that he

---

[2] I use the verb *to bite* here not in a metaphorical sense. A knife may be thought of literally as an evolution of our teeth that has taken place through the mind. A knife is a tooth we carry in our hands. In this way, the injury I sustained as a child may be compared to the accidental biting of one's own cheek. I still carry the scar.

[3] In January 1839, a brief notice appears in the journal of the Académie des sciences introducing the daguerreotype process. To encourage the French government to offer the process as a free gift to the world, Dominique François Jean Arago reminds officials of the fleet of artists Napoleon took to Egypt to record discoveries made during his campaign. The daguerreotype, he claims, would make the same undertaking less expensive and improve its accuracy and speed.

[4] The ape and the fig have carved their initials into our genes. We can trace all of our arts, of which memory is the first, back to the fragrance of dates—the fruit-eater and the invisible flower.

might kiss the maidservant—
a good trade to a four-year-old
and better yet when I find the fig
is not one but two, fresh fragrant
ripe purple, both of them.

Later, *I am shut up in a room*
for being naughty
and try to break the windows to escape,
but at the window, I get caught
in the view:
the sea.

We stayed there for weeks,
my family always in the background
where I can't make them out.

iii.

A cottage, inhabited by an old man
who used to gives us plums. His white beard
seemed to stretch to the floor.

What instinct—hunger, pleasure,
fear of death—grabbed hold of this scene?
The taste of plums, their rich indigo,[5]
and *an indistinct fear of the old man*

---

[5] Green is the primary colour from which all others descend. I am told that ancient Roman texts contain instructions for making purple dye from damascene skins. The ruins of their camps are littered with pits.

are locked in my mind.[6]

To get to the cottage, *we crossed
a broad stream in a carriage.
The white foaming water
made a vivid impression.*
I had heard stories
of people drowning.

---

[6] Memory uses light and sensation to make its pictures, then pours the solution down the drain.

Vanitas

Some other recollections are those of vanity, & what is odder a consciousness, as if instinctive, & contempt of myself that I was vain—namely thinking that people were admiring me in one instance for perseverance & another for boldness in climbing a low tree.

    Charles Darwin
    "Life. Written August—1838"

At the age of six, I crowned myself the Prince of Oranges
as well as Sheriff and Champion of the Mount.
I ruled over all of the fruit in the hothouse and many
of the apples in the orchard, especially the sweet ones.
Demonstrations of my speed attracted audiences
from as far away as Shrewsbury School, and it was
not uncommon for those in attendance to remark
that they had never before seen a boy run as fast as I did.
At the time, my eye was so sharp the rarest of birds—
pheasants, herons, dot-eared coquettes—
frequently revealed themselves to me as I took
solitary strolls along the Severn. Once,
a wild peacock even followed me home,
only to be chased away by Spark (my pet dog)
before anyone had a chance to observe the miracle.
I dabbled in botany, quickly mastering the most complicated
names of plants, both foreign and domestic. My talent
for gardening emerged the first day I put spade to soil.
Within a month, I could command the flowers

to change their colours—the crocuses and primroses
being particularly obedient. These feats were, of course,
lies, but recounting them to others gave me pleasure.
These inventions are still so vivid in my mind I could almost
fancy they were real, but I remember
I stammered when I spoke, couldn't say the words
white wine without stumbling into a fit of sneezing.
I was afraid of being attacked by dogs,
read adventure tales under the dining room table.
We are supposed to remember that life is emptiness—
that we should hold our hearts up to God.
But my mind gets so full I forget.

Death of My Mother

My mother died in July 1817, when I was a little over eight years old, and it is odd that I can remember hardly anything about her except her deathbed, her black velvet gown, and her curiously constructed worktable.

> Charles Darwin
> "Recollections of the Development of My Mind and Character"

Each night, I add a tool to the table.
A bottle of turpentine or laudanum, a brush,
damp cloth, bowls of water, paper fans,
a cup of crushed pearls, gold flakes,
and shavings of unicorn. I offer them up
to the still life hanging on the wall,
to the columbines and poppies that grow there,
as a cure for her silence
and for my forgetfulness. With all my strength,
I rest my grief on that bed. I hide it in the folds
of her gown.

The Game Book

I can say in my own favour that I was as a boy humane, but I owed this entirely to the instruction and example of my sisters. I doubt indeed whether humanity is a natural or innate quality.

>   Charles Darwin
>   "Recollections of the Development of My Mind
>   and Character"

There were a few years when I took up hunting like a profession—as if hired by a coalition of insects to clear the fields of marauding birds. I never went for a walk without a gun and a piece of string. Each kill was recorded as a knot and at the end of the day; the number of knots was added to a tally I kept in a book. I shot at everything—hares, pheasants, partridges, pigeons—and experimented with rats trapped at the Mount. At night, I studied, fell asleep in instruction manuals and handbooks only to wake up at dawn so eager to shoot that my finger was on the trigger before I was dressed. I practiced my posture in the mirror. Took aim at my eye.

I learned that for each animal there is a precise shot size that will kill it; never throw a boulder at a sparrow. Use a size too small and you will cause injury—break a wing and be forced to finish the bird with your hands. Too big and the target will explode into a hail of feathers. Only the exact size clears the mess.

I learned to kill quickly. Death should be merciful, gentle, like a puff of air. Living is what's violent—birth and the surgeon who carves up his feast of pain. I watched one try to separate a child from its arm once.

By the time I stopped shooting, the path of destruction that trailed behind my gun was only as thick as a string.

A Vague Picture of Ships

Nothing could have been worse for the development of my mind than Dr. Butler's school, as it was strictly classical.... Especial attention was paid to verse-making, and this I could never do well.

> Charles Darwin
> "Recollections of the Development of My Mind and Character"

The decorative arts disguise the beauty of function.
A teacup may resemble an ugly stepsister as long
as it keeps the serving hot and sits comfortably
in hand or saucer. Metaphor may run in my family—
turn trees into elephants and baboons into grandfathers—
but what do you do with poetic sense and no skill?
Given a quill and brought before a blank page,
I can use words but never make them.
The facts simply march out in single file, in uniform,
deserting the castles in my head, razing walls I have built
in my sleep. How do you fit the horizon between
the left and right margins? How do you see past words
to the vanishing point where letters converge
to form a feeling? No cave art was ever discovered
in England. Had it all washed away, or was it never there?
All that remains of Liverpool is a vague picture of ships
and a good dinner. Of the year my mother died:
the funeral of a soldier, his regiment firing at the sky.
At night, they will make a trophy of his ghost,
and I will watch birds in the sky close their wings,

let go of air, and feel what it's like to be a bomb.
They always land just as softly as the sound of that word.

The Laboratory

The fact that we worked at chemistry somehow got known at school.... I was...publicly rebuked by the headmaster, Dr. Butler, for thus wasting my time on such useless subjects.

> Charles Darwin
> "Recollections of the Development of My Mind and Character"

i.

Erasmus and I joined the chemical revolution,
claiming an old shed in the garden as our laboratory.

The room was humble. Underneath the rotting floorboards
there was no foundation. To prepare the way for experiment,

we overthrew the idols of philosopher kings and alchemists,
caught fire, air, earth, and water and threw each

into its own prison. With a wick, we tied flames to lamps
and limited their rations of whale oil. We called air

by its new names—nitrogen, argon, oxygen, carbon dioxide—
to anger it and let it know we were watching its movements.

Distilled water was placed in stopped bottles and made to work,
perform tricks for the benefit of science.

Raindrops that found their way through the roof
were rounded up and thrown into a barrel outside.

The old floorboards were ripped up and replaced
with solid English oak.

This action, supplemented by frequent sweeping,
kept the earth down.

ii.

Once order had been established, we hung the laws of the house
on the wall beside the Table of Simple Substances.

Slowly, a range of apparatuses began to arrive,
each pointing with a different finger towards discovery.

There were gifts—a thermometer, an Argand lamp—
and investments—a goniometer, a blowpipe.

From the glass house people
came jars, test tubes, and measuring equipment.

We picked up stopcocks and minerals along the way,
like loose change. At first, our experimental ventures

sought solids—we measured the angles of crystals, followed
their halls of mirrors toward well-defined principles.

Liquids passed through fingers too easily, escaped
out of unstopped bottles, were lost down drains.

And gases—it was enough to repeat the rumour:
they were there.

But soon the cold metals in our hands, despite their sparkle,
were too slow.

In a simple cup of water there were atoms   racing ahead,
daring us to catch them.

So we took the liquid, like a knot and untied its gases,
trapped them in glass nets

so we could see clearly, for the first time,
without a doubt in our minds, the seams of the universe.

NOTEBOOK M

People of the Paleolithic have very probably some two concepts, which change our vision of the world. They are the concepts of fluidity and permeability. Fluidity means that the categories that we have—man, woman, horse...tree, etc.—can shift. A tree may speak. A man may get transformed into an animal, and the other way around given certain circumstances. The concept of permeability is that there are no barriers, so to speak, between the world where we are and the world of the spirits—a wall can talk to us, accept us, refuse us....

    Jean Clottes, Former Head of Scientific Research, Chauvet Cave, *Cave of Forgotten Dreams*

And this our life...Findes tongues in trees, bookes in the running brookes, Sermons in stones.

    William Shakespeare
    As You Like It

Walking Palm

We apply the term walking *to these phenomena because of the leg-like action of the stilts and because the plant eventually straightens itself at a new location, but we do not mean to attribute purpose to the plants.*

> John H. Bodley and Foley C. Benson, Botanists
> "Stilt-Root Walking by an Iriarteoid Palm in the Peruvian Amazon"

Methought the wood began to move, and I asked who
would be killed. The trees do not mean to walk,

they said, it is an accident of evolution, of light
leaving them, of words belonging to a different kingdom.

walk: 1) to move at a regular and slow pace
by lifting and setting down each foot in turn.

walk: 2) to move at an irregular and very slow pace
by leaning and setting down new roots in turn.

A foot every two months—at this pace, the king will die
of natural causes.

What if I could only step once?
Where would I choose to plant my feet?

The sound of rootsteps threatens more than the withering
of the stilts left behind, marking the place where rootprints rest.

I would like to know whose funeral I am to attend.
The king's? The word's? The stilt's? My own?

The Treehouse

If the tree has no roots,
what will become of the house
I have built there? It cannot be
disassembled and carried on my back.
My body cannot support this shell.
You will protest: houses have never had
foundations. You will tell me: roots are built
in darkness so no one can see their fiction.
You followed the trunk into the ground
because the origin was a mystery,
and found that this truth alone remains
truth. I am not certain of anything without roots,
but I believe a tree without them is not a tree at all;
it is star.

      But I cannot live there. I would fall
through its branches. I would crumble in its heat.

Botanist Somnambulist

Palus Somni,

            lakes on the moon are like colours in a dream,
empty. If only the rain would come and fill them up.

The botanist somnambulist has made his bed
a boat. He is waiting on the grass by the shore
for the dream-crowned captain to take him to Greenwich.
Lying there in the sheets in the reeds in the dream,
he shows you all the names in his collection,
but he cannot tell you his own. Tonight, his mind
is a room I have stepped into, and you
are its only reflection. When the tide comes in,
it paralyzes the sleeper; when it goes out,
it exposes the dream. Seen from the lighthouse,
such ships are the poorest of countries. Take away
the stern, the bow, the hull—regions of material
and atmosphere—and you are left with a mast—
a tree shaved of branches, planted in the sand.

This must be the way we all looked
before we turned back, hoping for costume,
wearing nothing but air.

The Sleep of Leaves

It's not the darkness that excites them
but arithmetic—in a given day,
if the sum of light reaped
is greater than the sum of shadows,
the blades will rise up, under the stars,
and close their eyes.

      Only the shy ones
close altogether, folding themselves
along the midrib, the petiolule
into a contra dance of margins, of leaflets
into a cotillion of cotyledons, the facing lines
taking all night to move a centimetre
toward each other.

A slow ballet for the patient spectator
where the spectacle is not a loss of consciousness
but a single turn in a new direction.

Paper Birch

It's not fair to the tree if you only see yourself in it.
It's not a pond or a mirror. It doesn't *miss* the leaves
or *shiver* in winter.

In the *xylem*, *phloem*, and *cambium*,
I see no signs of life
except a kind of memory.

There is something familiar
in the double-toothed leaves,
in the drooping catkins (the yellow sons, the daughters green),
in the winged nutlets and bark, and the branches bending
but not enough.

But in the lenticels, those dry mouths
with an appetite for atmosphere,
I see a voice asking
to be left alone.

What the Earth Would Say

Sphagnum fallax, Cryphaea lamyana,
Equisetum pratense, Notholaena lemmonii,
Psilotum nudum, Ceratopteris richardii,
Taxus canadensis, Tsuga mertensiana,
Pinus ponderosa, Pinus banksiana,
Dracaena draco, Agrostis mertensii,
Olea europaea, Myrtus communis,
Pisum sativum, Salix matsudana,
Castanea dentata, Prunus persica,
Prunus avium, Linum usitatissimum,
Rubia tinctorum, Fagus sylvatica,
Haematoxylon campechianum,
Dactylopius coccus, Laccifer lacca,
Sepia officinalis, Nomen nudum.

Envy

The only colour I can see is human;
everything else is black.

I have been told there is such a thing as green.
I have been told there are people who see it,
but I don't know where to find them.

I am searching for a person who understands the trees.

Today, they are wintering, and winter is
black—a time when all shapes move into their stomachs
and wait inside their hunger.

I want green to come in its own image,

but I'm afraid I won't recognize it—
without leaves, branches fade into fingers.

I need something to speak between us.

I want to ask green what it is to be alive
without voice or eyes or sense of direction.
How do you know and remember?
Where do you keep your mistakes and your envy?

The trees can't watch, but they are watching me.
They are storing secrets inside their branches.
I want to know what they are thinking.
If I could only hear their thoughts, I could learn
how to be still. I could learn to be patient.

And for this and also if
they could hear me,
if I could know that they hear me,
I could teach them
how to walk away from the sun without dying.

Petrified Forest

These are the dead:

branches of government, the low ones that grew stunted
in the shade of the others

the forest, no one ever seemed to see

wooden objects in a million different rooms,
touched and knocked smooth
by anxious hands

the wrong tree, that fell
to silence so much barking

stump speech

root words

the new leaf, turned too many times over and over

All buried now
in the museum of metaphor.
Their graves are marked with pins.

M Is for Metaphor

If metaphor is a form of experiment,
I would like to use it to test a hypothesis:

that a bird is a cage for the sky.
Something has tunnelled through the bones of the finch.

To find out what I will ask
if there is a key that can open the bird

without breaking it. Is a knife a key? Is a pin?
Is there a lock hidden under all those feathers?

My results will show that knife and pin can open a lock
as small as a pore or as large as a beak,

but one opens too wide and the other just wants to fasten
the bird to the page. All I want to do is open and close,

find true and false. I will keep searching for the right key
to test my theory, because what else could have made the finch

more space than substance? What else
could give it the ability to fly?

M Is for Morality

The laws of planetary motion govern greater cosmic citizens.
With our feet on the ground, we are a little free
to move above them in erratic orbits.
But the laws of definite proportions,
constant composition, chemical equilibrium
are enforced inside every cell in our bodies,
inside every room or field we might enter.
Even a skydiver obeys gravity.
A scientific law holds its subjects in place,
making them perfectly predictable. In its fists,
our bodies bend as easily as starlight around the sun,
and we are free only to argue the length of our life sentence.
And yet, the law of the land is as brittle as a stone tablet;
the law of the sea is broken as often as the waves.

Type Specimen #1

Our letters have grown slowly. Over time, they have adapted to various writing techniques and tools, to the materials to be written on, to production techniques and prevailing styles—less in their basic structure than in their details. Changes have mostly occurred unnoticed and over long periods.

> Jost Hochuli
> *Detail in Typography*

Type Locality: The Roman Coliseum

Description: You are the kind of creature

a god would make to impress another,

the largest mammal on earth
    with a chisel for a father
    and a rock for a mother
that can carry the wonders of the world
on its shoulders.

In a voice that silences all others,
you disperse mercenaries and emperors,
promising to deliver their messages,
to skip them across centuries
before they sink in the rain.

Type Specimen #2

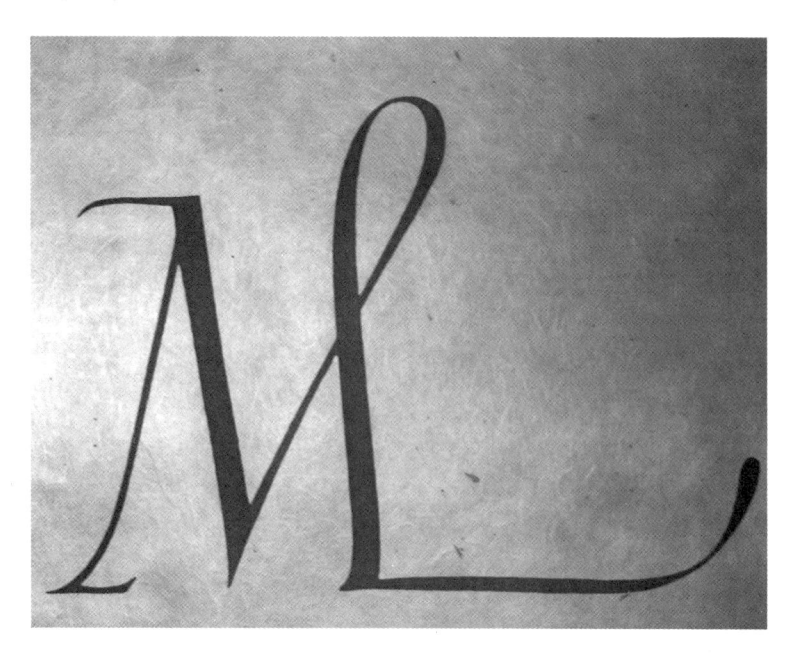

Type Locality: Jan van Krimpen Archive, Special Collections, University of Amsterdam

Description: Your ancestors were built for speed,
but over time, your feet grew tails.
A beak emerged from a shoulder,
an eye from another.

You should be grotesque,
should live hidden away underground
with many-fingered moles;
instead, you are prized
for the length of your stems

and the arch of your hairline.
Pens trace your curves on fine paper.
Collectors cut you out and hang you on the wall
above stuffed peacocks and blue-footed boobies.

You make poems want to stay on the page,
not care if they are ever spoken aloud.

Type Specimen #3

Type Locality: Yonge Street

Description: Fast growing, rapid reproducing,
high dispersal ability, phenotypically plastic,
ecologically competent, a generalist,
closely associated with humans.

You are invisible
until we notice
you are everywhere.

It's as if all our silk scarves
were carried away by the wind,
as if overnight all the leaves
on every tree in the city
turned into glass.
And we walk through the streets
with only a vague sense
that something is missing,
that we have seen the future.

M Is for Metaphysics

If you stretched its body out from end to end, it would wrap around the world an infinite number of times. And yet, the veins of its body carry no more blood than a pen carries ink. In the age of exploration, sailors setting out on voyages across the Pacific would pay a month's wages for a small vial of this blood, which could suppress the sensation of hunger, prevent a tattoo from fading, and, when mixed with salt water, become poison enough to end a long journey. For the last two hundred years, the species' existence was disputed. Taxonomists classified it in the genus *mythica* alongside the cinnamon bird and the griffin until it turned up on a remote island in the Atlantic, eating centipedes and fireflies and dandelion seeds. It has no wings, and the scattered pattern of its feathers, when seen from a distance, resembles granite.

M Is for Materialism

Collect coins, francs and those of roman ancestry. Collect seals, any you can peel off a letter or trace, ask for donations from family and friends. Collect pebbles and minerals and learn all their names, first and last. Fill your pockets with wildflowers, your books with leaves. Collect shells, antlers, the shed skins of snakes, lost teeth, tusks, claws, bones, and feathers. Collect insects—a Cimex, a Zygaena, a Cicindela—if alive, try to identify and draw them, then throw them back. Their lives are worth more than their names. Collect whatever you like that is dead—a pin can do no further harm. Collect newts and watch as they grow fresh legs. Collect habits—of starlings, robins, sparrows, peonies, gravel—and keep them in your notebook. Follow animals to their dens. If they keep you, the rest doesn't matter. If they don't, don't touch. Collect an egg from each nest you find, provided it contains more than one. With these things you can then build a shell, a soft one like a pea pod, or an eyelid that will harden into yourself.

The Empirical Disciplines

Sight: imperial empirical. But would you expect any less
from retina? Pupil? Iris? Listen to the I in the eye
and it will tell you where to find the focus.
This is the sacred space where only light can go.
This is where and how we think—the sense
that makes us trust the rest. It points and teaches,
keeps its distance, reaches out beyond our gadget fingers
and lets us know.

Touch: sense or violence? It's the one that bleeds
in extreme. If it's soft, it's a sensorium to be explored—
texture is a branch of cartography for the low impact
camper. But if it's hard, it's a blackout, one that rolls
slowly over you and straight to your head.

Taste: this is intimacy in infancy. The world becomes known
one *amuse bouche* at a time. But then the tongue starts twisting
and stops tasting. O psychoactive sense, if I could crawl
inside you, I would be complete. If I could be full
at the mouth, if my stomach didn't take you away and spoil
my appetite. You are the g-spot—the glottal stop.
I want nothing more than more of you.

Hearing: silence is freefall—the sleeper's suicide.
Here is the sense that guards the gates. Ears stand at attention
for good reason. We are lazy. We build them rigid
so they can weather the night without consciousness. And
that drum is a lighthouse while we dreamers are at sea, tossing,
unaware we might lose the life left on shore.

Smell: a place that arrives in you. A knock at your
septum brings you to stadium in seconds. Stench
hemorrhages where your memory is: at the brain stem.
Home of blood sport and botanics, bullrings
and sweet sweat. It is the guarded secret, the private part,
the only way back to the empirical here.

The Scientific Method

This is the equation for separating the observer
from the observed.
Cut off your nose. The sense of smell is worn out,
its findings too difficult to reproduce.
Tainted by memory, shaded by deep woods—
it is the source of epileptic seizures. Ask yourself:
what better way to streamline your profile?
Cut out your tongue. On long walks
you will need to keep your hands free
for lifting stones, pulling flowers. An empty mouth
provides storage space for specimens.
You won't even know they're there.
Cut off the tips of your fingers. They are too sensitive,
cause you to feel in the absence of stimuli.
This way you can hold all objects equally.
Cut off your ears. The world's ringing stops
and you are left in honest silence: science.
The yawn is a cry common to all mammals.
Now you can finally hear it.
Now you are all eyes.
Now your subject can be tricked into believing
you're not there.

M Is for Mania

...the only cure for madness is forgetfulness.

>   Charles Darwin
>   "Notebook M"

Before the world can be civilized, we must tame wonder.
A globe is the prison for it. Only a pin can pick the lock.
Shake an eye and the iris will shatter, filling the sclera
with its coloured flakes. A coat of arms is a scarecrow
you carry into battle to keep all the parts of yourself
together, to keep the enemy from growing on the field.
Where the soldiers fall, new ways of seeing will spring up.
And again and again the eye opens for the first time. In this war,
sight is a weapon of mass destruction and all survivors will
possess the bomb. All eyes sear the world differently.
The bull's eye, the bird's eye, the glass, compound, camera
naked, black. Prepare yourself for the path of enlightenment.

M Is for Memory

Now if memory of a tune & words can thus lie dormant, during a whole life time, quite unconsciously of it, surely memory from one generation to another, also without consciousness, as instincts are, is not so very wonderful.

>   Charles Darwin
>   "Notebook M"

Eventually, the earth forgets
in a sandstorm a speck of rock,
hushes and smoothes the place that said
here and how, and then
humans came along with a sense of wonder and
the habit of looking back.
What hasn't been found is a straight path leading to
the beginning is the end of the story,
and we're stuck holding an unmarked curve
of the plot. If you like the canopy now, the tree top,
the expensive view, you might ask: why go back?
And the orphans will say: because you are one of us
and they will dig down through the blankets
of sand the earth has laid over itself
and beg the secret to speak.
If it never does, the world is waiting.
But if you hear something,
it means the earth can remember
if only in pieces, if only in us.

The Dictionary

A is an ark entered, not just the animals entering. This ark is a
book: a bed of allegory where beasts become bestiary. The
cargo is inclusive: the Cheshire and the centaur beside the
dove and the donkey. The dinosaurs have died out but
enter through the exit. Extinction is etched on the sea
floor under fossil. F is for flora, fauna, and flood etched in
Genesis in Garamond or Gothic. Obey God and
He will hold you hostage, give you a hull-home and His word
in vermilion, in citrus, icteric olive, in indigo and violet.
Jehovah hangs his Jabberwock in the jet stream—and we
know it is a kite tethered to the keels of our feet.
Let us return to land; that is what this lifeboat is for.
    For looking up the
menagerie so it multiplies in our mouths and goes forth
not knowing its nearness to nova. To-night, all you nouns of
Oxford, rest your origins (in small caps) on old-growth
pulp. You have been pressed into pages by the lure of
quintessence. Remember there are three entries for *question*, and
    when the waters
recede, they will reproduce the Red Queen's race. Run,
Shakespeare, to the scriptorium if you want to save your
    monuments.
Turn away; the trope is stumbling. In the traffic
of usage is the making of meaning. A carriage waits, under
victoria. The vernacular is at war, and twenty volumes
have only enough room to hold the dead. Find the wall's
    weakness
and seep through. If you are X, escape to Xanada
and plant in the ground the only answer you are seeking: yes!

Tails, Pits, Beaks, and Wings

Coccyx is a white-coat word,
Greek for a cuckoo. *Coccyx* squawks
because an anatomist thought
the bone at the base of the spine
looked like a sort of bill.

Axilla is a name nostalgic for the early
Mesozoic when all chordates were created equal.
Before our could-be feathers fell out
and fingers made our wings different.

The vernacular is not so sentimental
and looks to the earth for inspiration:
tailbone and *armpit* are flightless words.

The tailbone is where our memories
of animality are stored.
It used to be filled with instincts,
but over the years, it got cut off
from the spinal cord.
Now the messages it tries to send to our busy brains
are often returned unopened.
They say the human race is getting taller.

And *armpit* has been wallowing in dirt
since it was first committed to paper.
You need only follow the prints
to find out where it began.

And yet the armpit is not such an unholy place,
a sort of archway where a tired lover can hide out.
If the hollow were only bigger,
if our bodies were only smaller,
our angels might be four-legged
and our dreams of crawling
instead of flight.

Blind Cave Fish

According to Darwin's view (since reaffirmed by a century and a half of further biological evidence), natural selection is a purposeless process but an efficacious one. Impersonal, blind to the future, it has no goals, only results.

>David Quammen
>*The Reluctant Mr. Darwin*

I found god in a cave full of dead things. I wasn't looking for him but crawled on all fours into a cavern as big as a cathedral with stalactite ceilings and a choir of bats, and I brushed my hands over the surface of a pool, and god swam up and sucked my fingers.

God is small and white and blind. Mostly he swims in circles and has no sense of direction. I asked him if he misses his eyes. There are other gods in the cave, but they are all the same. There is only one way to live in the dark, so there's no use in being different.

All the gods will live forever because there is no sun to weary them. The gods have forgotten the sun; they do not know they are fish.

M Is for Monkeys

The evolutionary show is over.
In the next millennium,
the most exciting thing
the human body will do is lose hair and shed toes,
molting its way forward and downward.
There's no going back to the trees,
but every morning I eat the same finger.
Not the little one or the middle or the ring,
not the index but the Cavendish. Bananas
may grow in bunches, but they are sold in hands,
and one digit is the same as any other. Thumbs
don't come from trees, and I wonder
how I would peel a banana
without one on each palm.
Do they taste good whole? I wonder
what I would eat, what I will eat
when there are no more bananas.
My sister washed all the lice
out of her hair, and my mother has never had ticks.
I am going to miss the banana—the perfect
fruitless fruit
with just a sterile fossil of seed inside it.
I am going to miss their potassium
and their sense of humour,
reminding us that we all fall
back to the ground we came from.

SOURCES

It would not have been possible for me to write these poems without reference to the following primary and secondary texts and websites.

Janet Browne's *Charles Darwin: Voyaging* (Princeton: Princeton UP, 1995) and *Charles Darwin: The Power of Place* (New York: Alfred A. Knopf, 2002); Charles Darwin's *Voyage of the Beagle*, edited by Janet Browne and Michael Neve (London: Penguin, 1989), *On the Origin of Species* (Cambridge: Harvard UP, 2003), and *Selected Letters on Evolution and Origin of Species*, edited by Francis Darwin (New York: Dover, 1958); *Charles Darwin's Notebooks*, edited by Paul H. Barrett et al. (New York: Cornell UP, 1987); *More letters of Charles Darwin: A record of his work in a series of hitherto unpublished letters*, edited by Francis Darwin and A.C. Seward (public domain); Darwin Correspondence Project (www.darwinproject.ac.uk); Darwin Online (darwin-online.org.uk); Lorraine Daston and Peter Galison's *Objectivity* (New York: Zone Books, 2007); Richard Dawkin's *Unweaving the Rainbow: Science, Delusion and the Appetite for Wonder* (New York: Mariner Books, 2000) and *The Ancestor's Tale: A Pilgrimage to the Dawn of Evolution* (Great Britain: Weidenfeld & Nicholson, 2004); Daniel C. Dennett's *Darwin's Dangerous Idea: Evolution and the Meanings of Life* (New York: Simon & Shuster, 1995); Jacques Derrida's "Eating Well, or the Calculation of the Subject," *Points...: Interviews, 1974-1994*, edited by Elisabeth Weber (Stanford: Stanford UP, 1995); Adrian Desmond and James Moore's *Darwin: The Life of a Tormented Evolutionist* (New York: Warner Books, 1991); David Quammen's *The Reluctant Mr. Darwin: An Intimate Portrait of Charles Darwin and the Making of His Theory of Evolution* (New York: Atlas Books, 2006); and Ruth Padel's *Darwin: A Life in Poems* (Great Britain: Alfred A. Knopf, 2009).

Acknowledgements

This book was written between 2005 and the summer of 2012. Several of these poems appeared in *Contemporary Verse 2* and *The Toronto Review of Books*. Thank you to the editors of these fine journals.

Thanks to Mike O'Connor and Dan Varrette at Insomniac Press; to my editor, Sachiko Murakami, for thoughtful edits, guidance, and friendship; to William MacIvor for insightful reading and conversation and for the beautiful cover design; to David McGimpsey, Mary di Michele, Stephanie Bolster, Judith Herz, Susan Gillis, Kate Hall, Jani Krulc, Anne Michaels, Moez Surani, and Steven Heighton, who read early versions of these poems and helped to shape their present form.

I owe a huge debt to Martine Garand, Curtis Pentland, Carolyn Smart, Mark Jones, Scott-Morgan Straker, George Logan, Jason Camlot, Jon Paul Fiorentino, and Bernard Schiff for good lessons, space and permission to be creative, and encouragement at key moments.

To dear friends in Vancouver, Edmonton, Winnipeg, Montreal, Ottawa, Toronto, New York, and Washington for distraction at key moments.

A very special thank you to Zachariah Schnier—these poems would be a messy heap of pages without you.

Thank you to Paul, Liz, Ellen, Michael, Niki, Adam, Ryan, Jaimie, Betsy, Rob, Romy, and Jeremy for all your support. And to my sisters, Meghan and Allison Savigny, and my parents, Margie and Wayne Savigny, for inspiration and for so much love!

And finally to a certain Mr. Darwin, whose public and private writing inspired this book.